Queen Things

Robyn Kelly

BookLeaf Publishing

India | USA | UK

Presentation by *BookLeaf Publishing*

Web: www.bookleafpub.com

E-mail: info@bookleafpub.com

ISBN: 9789358317855

First edition 2023

To the Kings and Queens—past, present, and future—who inspire me to not only survive, but to thrive.

ACKNOWLEDGEMENT

Words cannot express the gratitude I have for the friends, family, and perfect strangers who have supported me at my worst and celebrated me at my best. You're the real MVPs.

PREFACE

I am a daughter, friend, aunt, leader, woman, thriver. I am doing Queen things.

Although the details of this book are based on my individual experiences, the theme of each poem reflects aspects of a shared human experience. The highs and the lows. The good and the bad. The pain and the healing. The looking back and the moving on. The closure and the lack thereof. The love and the hate. The joy of living. Going into the depths instead of staying at the surface. Pushing myself out of my comfort zone. Being vulnerable enough to connect with others and saying "Me, too." Understanding who I have been and knowing who I want to be. Growing. Evolving. Finding the peace and power in saying this is not the end of my story.

Butterfly Memories

Childhood is like a butterfly—beautiful,
But escaping from you in the blink of an eye.
Freedom, like running on a playground,
Glides and propels
Through the winds of our minds.
The erratic images,
Shapeless and forgotten as we age,
Fluttering through the shadows of our past.
But for those of us
Who see through the darkness,
The fleeing images are never truly lost.
Flickering on the screen of our hearts—
Grainy memories repeating,
Keeping us held in a loop of time.
The theme songs, background noises,
And echoes of voices past
All blending together in narration.

Sit down and stay a while—
I want to remember just a little bit longer.

2

Fishing in a Bucket

It was a tradition for us,
A way to escape life for a while.
It was a bucket filled with water.
Oh, how he loved to fish.
It was more than a hobby,
It was a passion.
It was a way for him to find
Peace and solitude.
But what he grew in years,
He lost in strength,
And he could no longer
Fish the traditional way
In his favorite pond or lake.
So he filled a bucket with water,
Put it in his tool shop,
And we started fishing in a bucket
Together.
It was more than just playing around
With lures and lines.
It was more than catching pretend fish,
Or a way to pass the time.

It was a time for stories—
Stories about the past,
Stories about life,
And stories about fishing.

It was how an unbreakable bond
Formed between
A young girl and an old man,
It was fishing in a bucket.

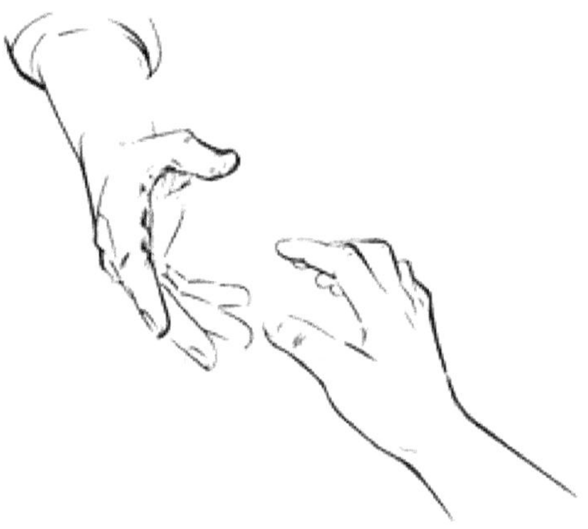

Character

The characters in my story are many.
Some are kings, some are queens,
And some are jokers.
Then there are the villains.
But my loyalty has always been
To the King.

He was a young man—
Not faultless,
But moral and accountable.
He is an old friend—
Standing firm
In loyalty and empathy.
He is a leader—
Decisive and protective,
The Great Stabilizer.
He will sacrifice himself—
Inspiring and blessing others.

Calm,
Honest,
Accepting,
Respectful,
Ambitious,
Compassionate,

Trustworthy,
Energetic,
Reliable—
This is how I remember him.

The King was traditionally successful—
Building an empire and a family,
But there were personality differences,
Jealousy, and ulterior motives.
There were cracks in the kingdom's façade
And the walls tumbled down.
All the makings of a plot twist.

Journey Through My Mind

Walking blindly through
The wilderness of my mind,
I stumble and fall over the debris
But pick myself back up.
Facing a narrow, crooked path
Of a strange kind,
As dazed and confused
As a newborn kitten.
I stumble and fall over the debris
But pick myself back up.
I fall again,
But refuse to give in,
As dazed and confused
As a newborn kitten.
I am followed by
A haunting past full of sin,
I fall again,
But refuse to give in,
An invisible force
Lifts me to my feet.
I am followed by
A haunting past full of sin.
An overwhelming presence,
Harsh but sweet.
An invisible force

Lifts me to my feet.
Facing a narrow, crooked path
Of a strange kind.
An overwhelming presence,
Harsh but sweet.
Walking blindly through
The wilderness of my mind.

The Day I Died

What is this venomous poison,
Seeping through the veins
Of a stiffened body
Cold to the touch?

Persistent in evading emotion,
Running from the monster inside
Screaming in agony,
Caused by desperation.

Emotions lack effect in this world,
For I am built with impenetrable stone
Where nothing can be seen
In this endless darkness.

Enveloped, surrounded, overwhelmed,
A taste of this poisoned apple
Becomes bittersweet
I feel nothing but am aware of everything.

Pretend detachment from this body—
Disengaging,
Escaping from torturous temperaments
A brief freedom replaced by the aroma of death.

Toxic Lover

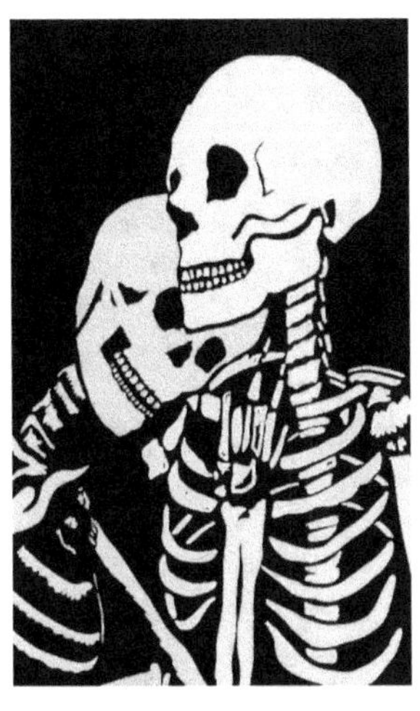

I thought our love was something special,
But you turned toxic today—
Swearing me to secrecy.
When all is said and done,
Would you still choose me?
Or does your pick of poison always win?

I want to be drug-free.

Your love makes me weak,
Flowing through my body,
Building up to the point of an overdose.
I was so sure you were worth the pain,

My drug of choice.
I tried to quit you, but your grip is strong.

I want to be drug-free.

How can you not see the damage you do?
Or is it that you never cared—
Is it all fair in love and war?
Your words are like needles
Poking into my skin.
Your apologies burn inside my veins.

I want to be drug-free.

I still want to believe there is a future,
But all I see is today.
A mangled mess of hopes and dreams
Passed out on the couch.
You may stand and stumble,
but we both will fall in this tragic affair.

I want to be drug-free.

I'm too old to live like this,
Too young to be this wise.
My heartbeat races faster
With the disappointment, the shame,
But I keep falling—falling back into you—
My toxic lover.

I want to be drug-free.

Old habits die hard.
Your poison lays next to you
On the floor—warm to the touch now.
She winks at me,
Knowing that she will betray you
In every way.

I want to be drug-free.

There is no rehabilitating us—
My heart finally bursts,
Our fairytale of everything that was
Bleeding out
Alone in the dark
I have nothing left to give

I want to be drug-free.

Heaven and Hell

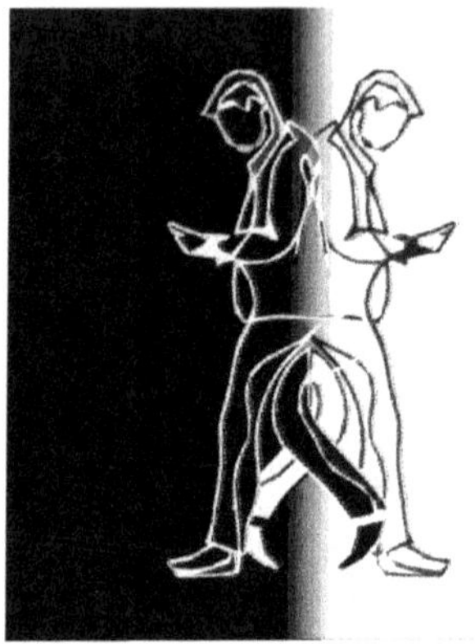

To the men I have known:

Some of you were Heaven on earth,
Safe places full of joy and acceptance.
My protectors and guardian angels.
But most of you were Hell itself.
And this caged bird forgot how to sing.
You dressed it up like the American dream,
With invisible locks in the trappings of a home.
I wonder if breaking my soul sounded like
The breaking of a bone—loud and sudden.
You lived your life as a ghost—
Not knowing where you wanted to be,
Floating through here, there, and in between.
A self-imposed purgatory of sorts.
If you don't want to be judged,

Then why do you do things in the dark?

Because of you,   15
I learned what love is.
Because of you,
I learned what love is not.
Because of you,
I know what love should be.

Abandoned

A "No Trespassing" sign was outside—
I ignored the red flag(s).
The yard was so enchanting—
Full of butterflies and lies.
Funny how you thought the grass
Was greener everywhere else,
But never bothered to water your own.

I helped you decorate this house
And make it a home.
A monster lives in there now—
He said he used to know you well.
Monsters aren't the same as beasts though,
And this beauty can't save you.

Here is the kitchen—
I used to cut myself here,
Making myself bleed the pain out,
To feel alive again for a little while.
Now, the cabinet doors are missing,
The wall calendar forever stuck in time.

Here is the dining room—
I used to eat here,
My favorite meal was steak.
You cooked it just the way you liked it.
Now, the chairs lie sideways on the floor,
The walls caving in.

Here is the living room—
I used to sit here,
Looking at the picture frames.
You never put pictures in them,
Keeping the store-bought families instead.
Now, broken glass shines in the sunlight.

Here is the bedroom—
I used to hold you here,
Through the sleepless nights,
When your demons raged,
Tossing and turning you all night.
Now, your pants are in the closet, wet from the
rain.

I don't live here anymore,
But this was never my home.
I walked out the door for the last time
In the winter.
It snowed at the beach that year.
Twice.
I guess Hell finally froze over.

The Aftereffects

The brain fog—I can't think straight,
I question myself, I question everything.
The trauma eyes—bloodshot and heavy,
Because I haven't slept in days.

The internalization—I have so many emotions,
That I just can't put any words to.
The isolation—I hide myself away,
My back hunched from the weight of secrets.

The anxiety—I obsessively clean the house,
Every day to feel some sense of control.
The wasting—I'm hungry but I don't eat,
Nothing tastes the same anyway.

The addictions—coping the best way I know,
But the highs never last.
The external validation—people tell me
You're okay, everything is okay.

The triggers—my heart races uncontrollably,
It's fight or flight all the time.
The exhaustion—my body is tired,
But there is no rest for my soul.

I hid it for so long,
I thought I could do it forever.
But people are starting to ask questions.
Are you okay?
We've noticed you aren't yourself.
We need to talk.
The intervention is coming.

Rose Colored Glasses

I can't see without my glasses.
You bought me a new pair—
Try them.
They were rose colored.

I put them on, and I saw you so clearly.
Handsome—we were like magnets.
You brought me flowers—white roses.
Charismatic—everyone knew you were there.
You promised me a future—restaurants, travel.
Protective—always checking on me.
You told me you would always be there.
A hustler working hard to do better.
You helped me focus on my goals.

The glasses started to slip one day.
I thought I saw something strange,
Out of the corner of my eye.
That can't be right though.

I took them off, and I saw you so clearly.
Ugly—you don't smile, you smirk.
You threw the next gift in the trash.
Insecure—you don't even love yourself.
You hated what you first loved about me.
Possessive—keeping me in a box all to yourself.
You left me for days, weeks on end—not a word.
A lazy person using others to get ahead.
You said nothing I did was good enough.

You insisted I put the glasses back on.
You said I looked better with them.
But I started getting migraines,
Everytime I wore them.

The glasses slipped down my nose again.
I thought I saw something else,
Out of the corner of my eye.
That can't be real though.

Your words finally hit me too hard,
And the glasses broke.
The lenses shattered into pieces,
All over the floor.

I finally saw the real you.
You were wearing a mask, all this time,
Hiding the truth—I was always better than you.

It is you. Not me.

I thought we were more alike than different,
Twin flames, soulmates, all the fairytale hype.
There was a time when I could have
Ended up just like you,
Moving from one person to another.
I actually tried it for a while,
No strings, no attachments, no emotions,
But I chose to understand my demons,
To accept them, to love them.
Because love always wins, right?

You became your demons instead,
But you can't even see the truth.
Your relationships are transactional,
Superficial at your best.

You're all talk—gimmicky enough
To be an infomercial personality.
Keeping up that image is hard though—
You left the price tag on your coat.
People told me you're a nobody.
I should have listened.

I was too good for you,
But I couldn't see it then.
My relationships are genuine, authentic,
A rare depth even at my worst.
I'm all action—I may not always say a lot,
But I'm the ride or die.
Keeping up this wall around my heart,
Is hard though—I feel too much.
People tell me I'm gorgeous, vivacious,
A real catch, and I should listen.

Be careful with your next move,
When you have a Queen in your hand.
Everyone you're chasing is a pawn,
And you can't afford impulsive distractions.
It's hard to make a move when you don't know
Who you are or what you want.
There is no knight in shining armor here,
This queen is three moves ahead of you.
You're in the Queen's Gambit now,
And this queen is the best you never had.

Karma

I have no taste for revenge anymore.
For what it's worth, losing me is enough.
You'll look for me everywhere you go,
But never find me again.
Forever haunted by memories, possibilities.

I can heal, you can't.
I can find joy, you chase momentary happiness.
I go out of my comfort zone and actually live,
You repeat the same cycle day after day,
Only switching out the players.

You can try to get your lick back,
My karma isn't payback though,
It's a comeback.

The Player's Club

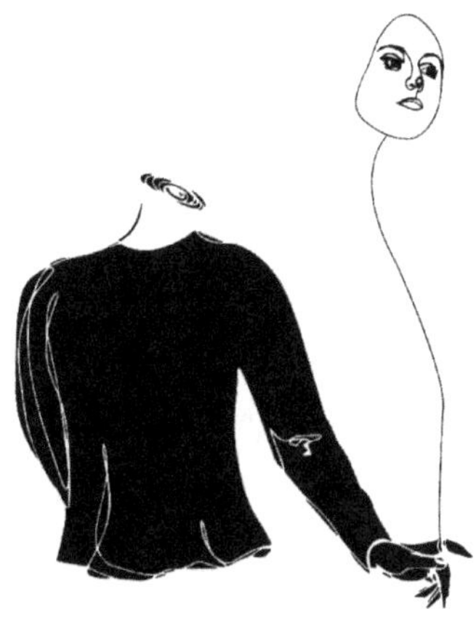

Someone once gave me a ticket,
To the greatest show on earth.
What a grand masquerade it was!
People dressed in their finest costumes,
A rainbow of ballroom gowns,
Against the black of tuxedos.
The music played, the dancers danced,
The sounds of laughter and clinking glasses.
I was pulled into a whirlwind of bodies,
Twirling, touching, sweating from the heat,
Slipping on the alcohol spilled all over the floor.
Everywhere I looked there was a different mask.
The animal.
The clown.
The ringleader.

The magician.
They were all there.
The world spun around me faster and faster,
Everyone pretended to be someone they weren't.
The masks blended together in a smoky haze.
The voices all talked over each other—
I'm the best! No, he's the best!
Lost in the illusion, the glitz, the glamor.
Who do you want to be today?
Pick your character.
Is this what you want?
The fakery and the fuckery?
I don't belong here.
This world is not for me.
I took my mask off and threw it on the floor,
Walking barefaced through the crowd.
Everyone stopped for my personal rebellion.
Now I was the main attraction.

Thank You

To the best friends, to the heroes,
To the new friends, to the whisperers,
To the loud ones, to the ones who want more,
To the listeners, to the negotiators,
To the feelers, to the thinkers, to the doers,
To the emotionally unavailable ones,
Thank you.

For holding me back,
For picking me up off the floor,
For creating the chaos,
For bonding with me over the trauma,
For pushing me over the edge,
For patiently waiting for me to live,
For the pain of lessons learned,
For the gift of laughter,

For showing me I deserve better,
For teaching me how to move on,
For the trials and tribulations,
For the affirmations and love,
For celebrating, not just tolerating, me.

Thank you for it all.

The Resilience

The cuts I made, the wounds you left,
All of the scars I covered with tattoos,
My story is written on my skin,
But this isn't the end.
All the noise, the voices in my head,
Screaming, cursing, name calling,
They speak softly now.
All the supply, the validation you needed,
Lying, cheating, living in hypocrisy,
They don't hurt me now.
All the breadcrumbs you fed me,
Promising more, giving none, avoiding shame,
They belong to someone else now.
I am good enough, always have been.
You just weren't good enough for me.
You underestimated me—
Taking my kindness for weakness.
I only grew stronger in all your silence.
I move forward with acts of intentionality,
Reframing, resetting, and refocusing.
The little Kings and Queens are watching,
Everything I am and do is for you.
I may stumble, I may trip, I may fall,
But I do not stay down—the pity party stops.
I put the pieces back together, one by one,

Better and stronger this time,
And mix in some newfound ones.
I have places to go and people to meet.

The Fury Dress

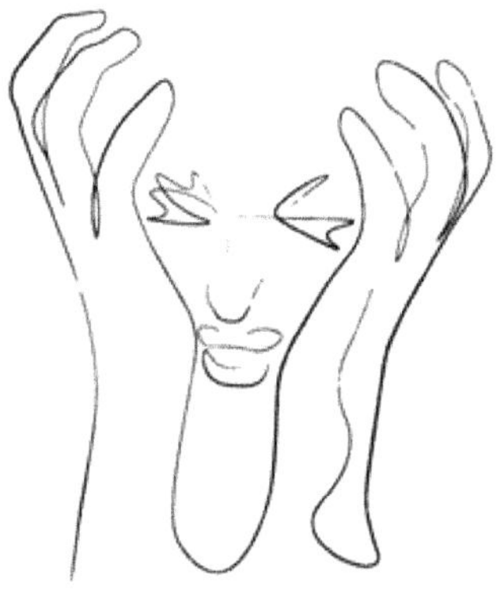

You lit my fuse and the anger ignited,
Your pile of lies and broken promises,
Made into the perfect kindling,
Growing each time you came back.

Every flame adding another layer,
Like tulle to this dress made of fury,
All of the negativity, trauma, and pain,
Blending together—yellow, orange, red.

Threads glowing through like embers,
The flames growing with shades of blue,
I saw you in the blue—your favorite color,
Watching me burn, adding fuel to this inferno.

I became the whole damn blaze in this dress,
The bridges I'm burning are shining bright,
Leaving nothing but a trail of ashes behind,
I'm moving on, moving forward, moving up.

I hope your gas lights are working,
The darkness will be overwhelming for you.

War

All you had to do was stay.
Instead you chose to run, to hide,
From me—
For making you feel things,
Vulnerability is too uncomfortable.
For holding you accountable,
Admitting the truth is too hard.
From yourself—
For not knowing who you want to be,
After those you loved abandoned you.
For being indecisive,
Nothing is ever good enough.

The day I snapped,
In the cry of battle,
All I wanted was revenge.

Your heart cut out of your chest,
But all you had was an empty space.
Your head on a stake,
Bad blood staining the ground.
Maybe poison was a better choice,
Adding that special ingredient,
To your favorite red velvet cake,
Violently putting you to sleep.
So many options in this personal vendetta.
My friends even took up arms,
Ready to go to war for me,
At the mention of your name,
At the first sign of disrespect,
Eyes up here, Sir.
They surrounded me like a wall,
Protecting me from all of the elements.
But not from myself.
Fake it until you make it,
Is bullshit advice.
Face it until you get through it,
I chose to fight the war within instead.

Now my revenge of choice is walking away,
Quietly, gracefully, indifferently.
There is poetry in my justice.

Skeleton Key

I know about the skeletons in your closet,
For everything that has life ends in death.

You do most of your deeds in the dark,
Always looking over your shoulder.

I sat by your side, silently watching you,
It's always the quiet ones you overlook.

I kept your secrets safe for you,
Wearing your skeleton key like a necklace.

Your Pandora's box of chaos is getting full,
And I'm finding that my voice has purpose.

Carousel

This ride is for your amusement,
Spinning round and round.
Each side piece a different animal,
Strategically placed just far enough apart.
It's hard to miss the elephant in the room,
Despite your best efforts to avoid accountability.
You really think you're in control of all this?
All that glitters isn't gold, but you can try it.
I hope you like the stain it leaves behind.

This ride is for our amusement,
Spinning round and round, faster and faster.
The colors blurring together like a rainbow,
Everyone watches you do your two-step shuffle.
Trying to keep up, trying to find the best seat,
Until you finally trip over yourself and fall.

Landing in the dirt beside this merry-go-round.
How does it feel to be on the outside looking in?
Unable to feel real emotion for any of us?

Puppet on a String

This is who I used to be,
A puppet on a string,
I belonged to you, not to me,
Another one of your objects, a thing,

Do you like how I dance?
Do you like the smile on my face?
When I jump and prance,
Filling the empty space.

Pull me to the left then the right,
Make me take a bow,
Push me down with all your might,
I am boring to you now.

Place me back on top of the shelf,
My wooden hands folded neatly,
Now you only possess yourself,
I've been cutting this cord so discreetly.

Whiskey Tea

This is who I am now.
There are times when I'm quiet,
There are times when I'm loud.
The context determines which is worse.

There are times when I'm strong enough to lead,
There are times when I'm soft enough to follow.
What you have to offer,
Determines which side you see.

There are times when I'm lost in the darkness,
There are times when I dance in the moonlight.
But I'll always thrive,
In the beautiful disaster that is life.

There are times when I dream of impossibilities,
There are times when I rebel against everything.

43

All I can do is wink at you
As I drink whiskey from a teacup.

Juxtaposition

There she is.
I finally found her.
Buried beneath the rubble.
I am your dream come true,
And your biggest nightmare.
I am the calm before the storm,
And the hurricane.
I am a culmination of every
Person, place, and memory gone by,
I am everything you said
I shouldn't (couldn't) be.
I am everything you tried to take (break)
And everything you never knew.
Everything you thought was too weird,
(You were too rigid),
Everything you thought was too clingy,
(You were too separated),
Everything you thought was too vulnerable,
(You were too scared),
Everything that was too this, too that, too much,
(You were never enough)
This is my voice,
(Your opinion means nothing),
This is my time,
(You had enough of mine),

This is my turn,
(You took my all and wanted more),
This is where I leave you behind
To follow a different path.
But this is not the end of my story.
I am here now.
I finally let go.
I don't have time to waste.

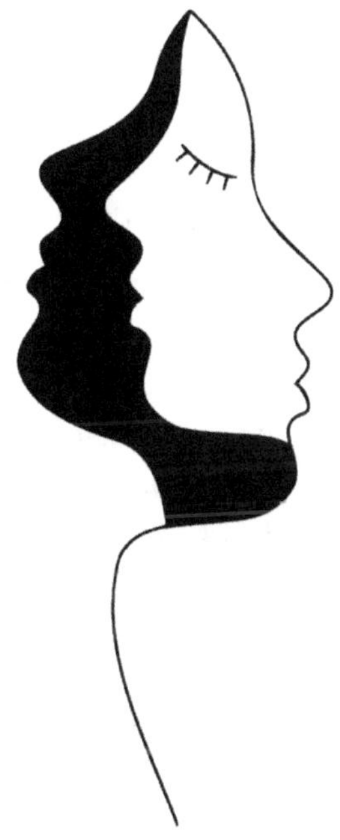

Colors

Color is my favorite.

Hot pink for my childhood bedroom,
Like the bubblegum I always chewed,
Like the birthday balloons at my party.

Blood red for all the love I have felt,
Like the hearts I drew on my homework ,
Like my fingernails dragging down your back.

Yellow for the uncertainty at times,
Like the traffic sign by the fork in the road,
Like the caution tape covering your door.

Teal for the renewal process I'm undergoing,
Like the ocean waves crashing on the shore,
Like the swallowtail butterfly in the garden.

You see life in black and white,
All or nothing.
I live in shades of gray,
The shadows of my freedom to choose.

Riding into the Sunset

It's a race to see who can move on the fastest,
Hurry up and start your engines!
Find the next person, place, thing you can use.
There's no time to waste!

Side by side we sit, revving our engines,
With a flip of the helmet visor down,
And a wave of the checkered flag,
Put the pedal to the metal and we're off.

For a moment, I wanted to ride with you again,
Turn your Hellcat around and pick me up.
I'm standing in the dust storm you left behind,
Remembering the good times we had in the car.

But I realized it was me that made this great,
Just me, not you—looks are deceiving here,

All you can offer is a passenger seat,
And I am meant to be more than a princess.

True healing takes time.
You will always beat me in this race.
I may be waving my white flag,
But you will never win peace.

Letting You Go

I am letting you go is easy to say,
But much harder to do.
I thought I succeeded so many times,
But found failure more often.
I wrote a list of all the ways you hurt me,
And watched it burn in the fire,
But I still remembered everything about you—
The way you felt, the warmth of your breath,
Everything.
I wrote you a goodbye letter and tossed it out,
When I jumped out of a plane,
But I still remembered everything about you—
The way you smiled, the sound of your voice,
Everything.
I purged each memory and thought,
Filling journal after journal,
But I am bonded to the trauma,
Ruminating over everything about you—
The insecurity, the jealousy, the projecting,
The hypocrisy, everything,
The future faking, the silent treatment,
The breadcrumbing, everything,
The lying, the disrespect, the insults,
Everything,
Everything that led me to find therapy—

Counseling, the gym, and finally, the wind.

I started riding a motorcycle last Summer.
I am free here—free of you, free of thoughts,
free of everything.
There is finally peace in letting you go.

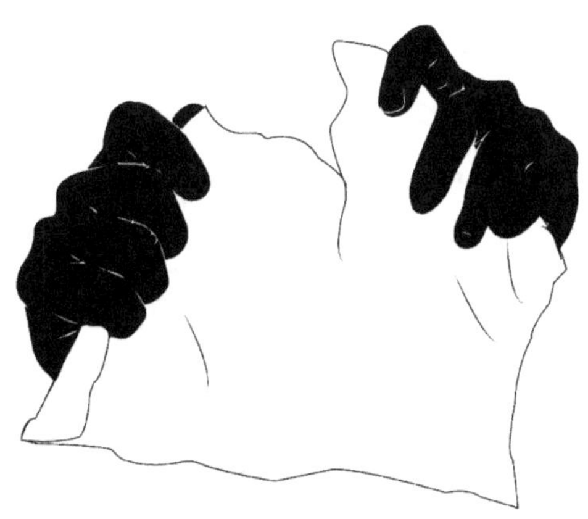

Block Party

I threw a party today to celebrate
The gift that is goodbye.
Some endings are necessary,
But I don't owe you an explanation.
You already crossed every boundary
I ever placed.
Even if you get past one now,
There is another one to cross.

Welcome to the gauntlet—a maze
Made of consequences for your actions.
At every turn, you have a choice to make—
Left or right?
Accept the challenge around the corner
Or hold on to your cowardice?
Look in the mirror and face yourself
Or deflect the questions like usual?

Your toxicity is no longer welcome—
This is a block party.
I am surrounded by people
Who are good to me and good for me.
You don't belong here anymore—
You never did.
No one will give you directions

Or help you find your way back here.

This party isn't about you.
It's about me.
I'm the one that got away.
It's my turn.

Words of Wisdom for my Mini Me

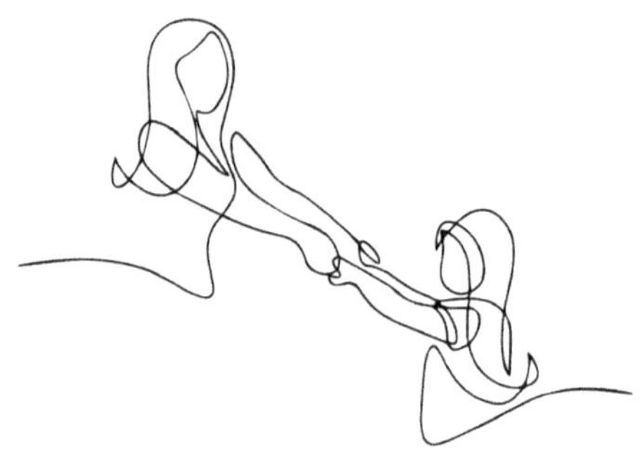

Not everyone you meet will be good to you,
Be good to yourself.
Do not fear the unknown,
Learn to trust yourself.
Not everyone will listen,
Find your voice and speak your truth.
Do not chase money,
Use it to fund your independence instead.
Not everyone will believe in your dreams,
Smile at them and do it anyway.
Do not hold onto the past,
Focus on a future that is so much brighter.
Not everyone will support you,
Have the tenacity to succeed anyway.
Do not fear the chaos,
Survive it until you can thrive in it.

Not everyone will understand how you made it,
But your resilience is undefeated.
Do not follow the pack,
You were born to find your own path.

You will never have it all figured out,
But don't you ever settle for less.

Good morning, Gorgeous!

Here's to the hustle and glow of a new day,
A day to start fresh, to do better than yesterday,
A day to love yourself just a little bit more,
To love the good, the bad, and the ugly,
All of the imperfections and the scars,
And the pieces that don't fit together so nicely,
Some pieces are sturdy—
Held together with glue,
While others move freely—
No amount of tape will do,
Everything is exactly as it should be though,
You are here at this moment for a reason.

Requirements

Wyd, wya, fml—this is dating now?
I am done with the time wasters,
I am done with the last minuters,
I am done with the skirt chasers,
I am done with the image fakers,
I am done with the dick swingers,
You think you have something to offer,
But leave empty handed.

I'll be the 10, you be better than a 6,
And I come with requirements,
Not expectations, requirements.
Don't put the ball in my court,
I have no room for games here.
Come at me correct, evolved/evolving,
Or keep it moving to the next.
I deserve it all after so much bad.

Love Poem

By your side (with you)
I remember sitting in your truck hat rainy night,
Holding so tightly onto the present you brought,
Listening to a song about porcelain on repeat.
Oh, the irony of that memory's soundtrack.
Everything felt right,
But wrong at the same time.
We talked on the phone for hours,
But you didn't know me.
You were too fixated on liking
How good I made you look.
You met my friends and family,
But they didn't care for you.
I ignored the comments,
The questions,
The are you sures.
I could have loved you so much,
But you wouldn't let me.

I thought you were worth the wait,
Worth the effort,
But I lost myself
In the thoughts of what could be,
Not reality.
Wearing that Black Dahlia smile
Like a badge of honor.
My happiness was so forced
It made the whole story fake.
I gave you everything
In return for nothing,
I must have been crazy,
Not in love though.
You showed me everything love is not.

By your side (with someone new)
Now I am with aman
Who looks like a bad boy,
Covered in tattoos and tattered edges,
But he has a genuine heart
Open to the vulnerability of love.
Now I am with a man
Who has a past,
Full of ups and downs,
Rights and wrongs,
But he has learned the lessons
And done the work to heal,
To evolve into a better version.
Now I am with a man

Who knows who he is—
No shapeshifting
Or moving the goalpost,
But he is open to learning new things.
Now I am with a man
Who knows what he wants,
A true hustler who does the work,
But understands work-life balance,
And knows the value of a lazy Sunday.
Now I am with a man
Who may not be the center of attention,
But he is no wallflower—
His quiet sense of humor lights the room up.
Now I am with a man
Who talks the talk
And knows there is power in his words,
But he also walks the walk,
Living a life of integrity and morality.
Now I am with a man
Who can lead by example,
Who can make informed decisions,
This man adds value to my life
In a way that lets me be softer,
This man reciprocates my effort
In a way that lets me relinquish control,
This man provides a safe place
In a way that makes me stop running.
This man shows me
Everything love is supposed to be.

9 789358 317855